SQL

*The Comprehensive Beginner's Guide to Learn SQL
with Practical Examples*

owen kriev

SQL: The Comprehensive Beginners Guide

Table of Contents

Chapter 1: Introduction

About SQL

Structured Query Language (SQL), is a computer language used for interacting with databases. The American National Standards Institute recognizes SQL as the standard language for relational database management systems (RDBMS). It is used to access, store, retrieve, and manipulate data stored in the form of tables within database system.

Initially, SQL was called SEQUEL. The official pronunciation, however, is ESS QUE ELL.

Why Use SQL?

A database language serves two essential purposes: to create, edit, and maintain a database and to perform queries. SQL and SQL-based applications have been accomplishing these tasks with efficiency and ease over the years. No computer language or application comes close to its features and capabilities in handling databases.

What makes SQL the language of choice for databases?

SQL has maintained its status as a standard for database language while competitors have come and gone through the years. It continues to work behind the scenes to improve database interfaces and to become even more responsive to the needs of its loyal users.

SQL is easy to use, powerful, and highly functional.

This database language has a simple structure. It uses few commands and conventions. Its command structure is limited to definitional and manipulative statements. The commands even use simple English words such as Create Table, Alter Table, and Insert into. Its statements are written in free format.

SQL is easy to learn and use. Its implementation will not require intensive training time and cost. Its intuitive command structure helps users at any level to familiarize themselves with the fundamentals quickly and easily.

SQL enables a large segment of an organization to efficiently optimize existing data for querying, data manipulation, and decision-making.

This powerful yet accessible database language is capable of meeting the requirements of management, employees working with data, and database administrators.

Every database application today is practically powered by SQL. Developers are proactively customizing the language to suit their requirements and this has resulted in the multiple variations and implementations of SQL. In spite of its continuous growth, SQL versions have remained anchored on the standard ANSI-SQL adopting slight variations only to conform to the specific needs of the market. This universality makes it simple to migrate from one database application to another without disrupting the underlying structures.

SQL has no major competitor at this point. Hence, you can expect it to remain the standard for relational database management and implementation in the years to come.

RDBMS

A database is an organized mechanism that you can use to store and access data efficiently. An example of a database is a telephone directory. A telephone directory typically contains information such as people's name, address, and phone number. The entries are generally presented in alphabetical order which makes it easy to search for the information that users might need.

A relational database is a collection of related information that are organized into tables. Data is stored in a table which consists of rows and columns. The tables are stored in database schemas.

Dr. Edgar F. Codd introduced the concept of relational databases in the 1970s while he was working as an employee at IBM. IBM released System R based on his database model. However, it was the Oracle Corporation that marketed the first SQL which was called the ORACLE database.

RDBMS stands for Relational Database Management Systems. RDBMS allows businesses and organizations to efficiently and effectively manage complex information and large amounts of data. SQL is the most commonly used language to access relational databases. There are several implementations of the SQL language and while all of them support the same SQL standards, they may come in different flavors and nuances.

The following are the most widely used RDBMS:

- MySQL

MySQL supports multiple platforms such as MS Windows, Mac OS X, and UNIX. It is commonly used with PHP for web development. Now owned by Oracle Corporation, MySQL offers both open source or community version and commercial version.

- SQLite

SQLite is an open source SQL database system which is capable of storing a database in a single file. It is commonly used in database for gadgets such as smartphones, PDAs, and MP3 players.

- PostgreSQL

PostgreSQL is more associated with web applications development. It is reliable, free, and easy to use. However, it is relatively slower and has fewer users than MySQL.

- Oracle DB

Oracle DB offers integrated business applications to manage the complex database requirements of large organizations. It supports all popular operating systems for servers and clients. It is a commercial database system owned by Oracle Corporation.

- MS SQL Server

MS SQL Server was created by Microsoft and only offers support for Windows OS. Its main query languages are ANSI SQL and T-SQL. It is a commercial database system.

- MS Access

MS Access is a Microsoft product that can be used to handle basic database operations. It uses a distinct SQL dialect called Jet SQL. MS Access has powerful features that are great for managing small-scale database requirements. It is also inexpensive.

What is a Schema?

A schema is a set of database objects associated with a specific user of the database. There may be several schemas in a database but each username is only linked to a single schema. A user controls the database objects linked to his/her name. Whenever a new object is created under the username, it is created under the user's own schema. Based on the privileges granted, a user has control over the objects that he creates, removes, or manipulates.

For example, assume that the database administrator has just granted your login credentials which you will use to access the XYZCOMPANY database. Your username is USER20 and you used this username with the corresponding password to create a table named EMPLOYEES within the XYZCOMPANY database. In the records of the database, you have just created a table with a filename of USER20.EMPLOYEES_TBL. The table has a schema name of USER20 which corresponds to the username of the creator of the EMPLOYEES_TBL.

When accessing data associated to your username, you can opt to use or not use the schema name. For example, there are two ways for you to access the EMPLOYEES_TBL:

USER20.EMPLOYEES_TBL
EMPLOYEES_TBL

On the other hand, other users will have to use the schema name to make a query on the table that you have created.

Because the schema name is actually part of a table's name, there can be tables with the same name within the database as long as each table belongs to a different user or schema. In reality, each table is unique because the schema name forms part of the table's name.

When accessing tables, bear in mind that if you don't specify a schema name in your query, the database server will initially search for the table under your schema name.

What is a Table?

Tables are the main data storage tool in modern databases. A relational database system may have one or more tables and they are used to hold the data for the database. A table is formed by columns and rows.

Here is a sample table named CUSTOMERS:

ID	NAME	AGE	LOCATION	SALES
1	Jack James	29	Oklahoma	5000.00
2	Mark Trevor	41	New Jersey	6000.00
3	Jane Philips	24	California	3300.00
4	Naomi Bills	98	Illinois	4200.00
5	Carl Moon	32	Utah	3500.00
6	John Jones	55	Nevada	4200.00
7	Jenna Queens	21	Oklahoma	3300.00

The column names are ID, NAME, AGE, LOCATION, and SALES. The rows are the related data which are arranged horizontally.

What is a Record?

A record refers to a related row of data in a table. For example, a row in the CUSTOMERS table above consists of related data for a customer such as the ID, name, location, and sales data. Rows are made up of fields that hold information for a single record in a table.

To illustrate, here is a row in the CUSTOMERS table:

1	Jack James	29	Oklahoma	5000.00

What is a Column?

A column stores all the data for a specific field. A column in a database table is specified with a column name, data type, and other attributes. A table should have at least one column.

The following are the column names of the CUSTOMERS table:

ID	NAME	AGE	LOCATION	SALES

What is a Field?

A field is the intersection of a column and a row. Hence, if your table has 5 columns and 5 rows, it has 25 fields. When you use the DDL statements to create a table, you are defining the columns and their attributes. When you add data to the rows, you are defining the rows and the fields. A table should have at least one field which is used to store a specific data type.

The following segment of the CUSTOMERS table shows the column names and a single row of data. One example of a field would be the space that contains the data Jack James which is stored under the column NAME and ID 1.

ID	NAME	AGE	LOCATION	SALES
1	Jack James	29	Oklahoma	5000.00

SQL Syntax

SQL syntax refers to the set of rules and conventions that govern how SQL codes should be written and interpreted. SQL has very simple syntax rules.

Databases processes valid SQL statements and execute them accordingly. An SQL statement starts with a keyword. In most SQL implementations, a semicolon is required at the end of a statement. When the database system allows the execution of multiple commands in a single call, a semicolon also serves as a separator between statements.

A statement consists of the following parts:

1. *A clause*

Clauses are commands that are used to perform SQL tasks. They are conventionally written in uppercase letters.

2. *Table name*

The commands are applied to the table specified in an SQL statement.

3. *Parameter*

The parameter refers to the columns, data types, and values that are passed as argument.

Example:

(column_1 data_type, column_2 data_type, column_3 data_type)

SQL statements have flexible structures. You may write a statement in a single line or in multiple lines.

Here are some examples:

CREATE DATABASE database_name;

```
CREATE TABLE members (
 id INTEGER
 name TEXT
 age INTEGER
 );
```

```
DELETE FROM table_name
WHERE {CONDITION};
```

ROLLBACK;

SQL is not case-sensitive. While the convention is to write the commands in uppercase, you may opt to use a keyword in either uppercase or lowercase. For instance, you can either write CREATE TABLE or create table when you want to create a new table.

Chapter 2: SQL Data Types

The data type attribute specifies the type of data that will be placed inside a database table. A data type is an attribute of the information itself. You will use this attribute to create a table that will be responsive to your needs. Additionally, the data type defines the type of operations that can be performed on a value or data.

Each SQL version has its own set of data types. You may need to learn the data types that are specific to each version to be able to effectively manage and optimize your database.

Most SQL implementations support the following categories of data types:

Character String Data Types
Unicode Character Strings
Binary Data Types
Exact Numeric Data Types
Approximate Numeric Type
Time and Date Data Types
Boolean Data Types

Character String Data Type

The string data type includes CHAR, VARCHAR, and TEXT.

CHAR(X)   This string type consists of a fixed length non-Unicode characters with a maximum length of 8,000 characters. The X parameter defines how many characters it will store. The data entered is right space-padded to fit the number of characters defined.

VARCHAR(X)   This string data type holds non-binary strings with variable length up to a maximum of 8,000 characters. The values are not space padded and are stored and displayed in the same format. The X parameter specifies the number of characters it will store.

TEXT   The TEXT data type holds non-binary strings of variable length up to 2,147,483,647 characters at the most. The other variants of the TEXT data type and their maximum length are as follows:

TINYTEXT   255 charracters
MEDIUMTEXT   16777215 characters

LONGTEXT   4294967295 characters

Unicode Character String Type

nchar   This is a fixed length Unicode type with a maximum length of 4,000 characters.

nvarchar   This is a variable length Unicode data type with a maximum length of 4,000 characters.

ntext   This is a variable length Unicode type with maximum length of 1,073,741,823 characters.

Binary Data Types

BINARY   Binary is a fixed length binary data with a maximum length of 8,000 bytes.

VARBINARY	Varbinary is a variable length binary data with a maximum length of 8,000 bytes.
VARBINARY (max)	This is a variable length binary data with a maximum length of 231 bytes.
image	This is a variable length binary data with a maximum length of 2,147,483,647 bytes.
BLOB	A BLOB or Binary Large Object refers to a data type that can hold large amounts of data, media files, or documents. Here are the types of BLOB and the maximum length that they can contain:

BLOB	65,535 bytes
TINYBLOB	255 characters
MEDIUMBLOB	16,777,215 characters
LONGBLOB	4,294,967,295 characters

String Functions

SQL supports the following string functions:

LEN ()

The LEN() function is used to return the length of text values.

Standard syntax:

SELECT LEN(column_name) FROM table_name;

Syntax for ORACLE

SELECT LENGTH(column_name) FROM table_name;

MID ()

This function is used to slice characters from a field with text values.

Standard syntax:

SELECT MID(column_name,start,length) AS some_name FROM table_name;

SQL Server syntax:

SELECT SUBSTRING(column_name,start,length) AS some_name FROM table_name;

ORACLE keyword for extracting a substring:

SELECT SUBSTR(column_name,start,length) AS some_name FROM table_name;

UCASE ()

This function is used to convert a field value to uppercase.

Standard syntax:

SELECT UCASE(column_name) FROM table_name;

SQL Server syntax:

SELECT UPPER(column_name) FROM table_name;

LCASE ()

This function is used to convert a field value to lowercase.

Standard syntax:

SELECT LCASE(column_name) FROM table_name;

SQL Server syntax:

SELECT LOWER(column_name) FROM table_name;

Numeric Types

All numeric types have a precision value. This value indicates the total significant digits of a number. Numeric types also have an optional scale value which indicates the position of the least significant digit to the right side of the decimal. For instance, the number 179876.54 has a precision of 8 and a scale of 2. You may define it as DECIMAL(8,2).

Exact Numeric Data Types

SQL supports exact numeric data types such as Integer and SMALLINT as well as some extension integer types.

This table shows the exact numeric types with their corresponding range:

Integer Type	Minimum	Maximum
INT	-2147483648	2147483647
TINYINT	-128	127
SMALLINT	-32768	32767

MEDIUMINT	-8388608	8388607
BIGINT	-9223372036854770000	9223372036854770000
SMALLMONEY	-214748.3648	214748.3647
MONEY	-922337203685477.5808	922337203685477.5807
DECIMAL	-10^38 +1	10^38 -1
BIT	0	1

INT/INTEGER

The INT type is an exact number type that uses decimal or binary precision. It always has a scale of zero and has minimum and maximum precision.

Usage: INTEGER(precision)

SMALLINT

The SMALLINT is an exact number type that uses decimal or binary precision. It always has a scale of zero. Its maximum allowed precision is equal to or less than an INTEGER's maximum precisions.

USAGE: SMALLINT(precision)

DECIMAL

The DECIMAL numeric type is a fixed-point type that you can use to work with exact numeric values. For example, the statement DECIMAL(8,2) is an SQL statement that defines a column with a precision of 8 and scale of 2. This means that it will store numeric data with 8 digits and 2 decimals. If you don't specify a value, it assumes the default value of 10. When the scale has no value or has zero value, it means that the number has no decimal or fractional part. A decimal data type can contain up to 65 digits.

Approximate Numeric Data Type

SQL supports the following approximate numeric types:

REAL

A real number is an approximate numeric type which uses binary precision.

FLOAT

A float is an approximate number type which uses binary precision when rounding.

Usage: FLOAT(precision)

DOUBLE PRECISION

Double precision is an approximate numeric type that uses binary precision. It's default precision should be greater than what is set for the REAL number.

Usage: DOUBLE PRECISION

Time and Date Data Types

This category includes the following data types:

DATE
TIME
DATETIME
YEAR
TIMESTAMP

DATE

The DATE type stores the year, month, and day and is used when you only want the date value. The date is displayed as YYYY-MM-DD and can range from from '1000-01-01' to '9999-12-31'.

TIME

The TIME data type holds the hour, minute, and seconds values.

DATETIME

The DATETIME type is used when you need both date and time values. It is displayed as YYY-MM-DD HH:MM:SS. Its value can range from '1000-01-01 00:00:00' to '9999-12-31 23:59:59'.

YEAR

The YEAR is used to store and display year values. Its syntax is YEAR() and you can either declare YEAR(4) OR YEAR(2) to display the year value in four or two characters respectively. The default width is four characters. In a four-digit format, the YEAR is displayed as YYYY with possible values from 1901 to 2155. In the two-digit format, the last two digits of the YEAR values are displayed.

TIMESTAMP

TIMESTAMP stores the combination of date and time and is a temporal data type. It is fixed at 19 characters and takes the format YYYY-MM-DD HH:MM:SS. Its value range from 1970-01-01 00:00:01 UTC to 2038-01-19 03:14:07 UTC.

Boolean Data Type

The Boolean data type consists of the logical true or false values. In PostgreSQL, it takes a third state: 'unknown'. The NULL value is used to represent this data type. There is no built-in BOOL or BOOLEAN data type in MySQL. The TINYINT(1) data type is used to represent BOOLEAN and BOOL.

Miscellaneous Data Types

`uniqueidentifier`

This data type is used to store a GUID or globally unique identifier.

`xml`

This is used to store XMLdata.

Chapter 3: SQL Constraints

Constraints refer to the rules or restrictions that will be applied on a table or its columns. These rules are applied to ensure that only specific data types can be used on a table. The use of constraints helps ensure the accuracy and reliability of data.

You can specify constraints on a table or column level. When constraints are specified on a column level, they are only applicable to a specific column. When they are defined on a table basis, they are implemented on the entire table.

SQL offers several types of constraints. Following are the most commonly used ones:

PRIMARY Key
FOREIGN Key
UNIQUE Key
INDEX
NOT NULL
CHECK Constraint
DEFAULT Constraint

PRIMARY Key

A Primary Key is a unique value which is used to identify a row or record. There is only one primary key for each table but it may consist of multiple fields. A column that had been designated as a primary key can't contain NULL values. In general, a primary key is designated during the table creation stage.

Creating a Primary Key

The following statement creates a table named Employees and designates the ID field as its primary key:

```
CREATE TABLE EMPLOYEES (
       ID  INT      NOT NULL,
       EMP_NAME VARCHAR (30)     NOT NULL,
       AGE  INT     NOT NULL,
       LOCATION  CHAR (30) ,
       SALARY   DECIMAL (12, 2),
       PRIMARY KEY (ID)
);
```

You may also specify a primary key constraint later using the ALTER TABLE statement. Here's the code for adding a primary constraint to the EMPLOYEES table:

```
ALTER TABLE EMPLOYEES
    ADD CONSTRAINT PRIMARY (ID);
```

Deleting Primary Key Constraint

To remove the primary key constraint from a table, you will use the ALTER TABLE with the DROP statement. You may use this statement:

```
ALTER TABLE EMPLOYEES DROP PRIMARY KEY;
```

FOREIGN Key

A foreign key constraint is used to associate a table with another table. Also known as referencing key, the foreign key is commonly used when you're working on parent and child tables. In this type of table relationship, a key in the child table points to a primary key in the parent table.

A foreign key may consist of one or several columns containing values that match the primary key in another table. It is commonly used to ensure referential integrity within the database.

The diagram below will demonstrate the parent-child table relationship:

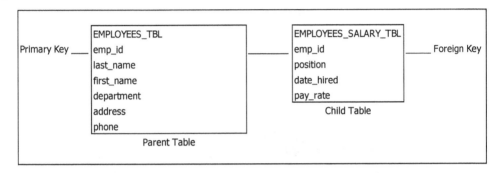

The EMPLOYEES_TBL is the parent table. It contains important information about employees and uses the field emp_id as its primary key to identify each employee. The EMPLOYEES_SALARY_TBL contains information about employees' salary, position, and other details.

It is logical to assume that all salary data are associated with a specific employee entered in the EMPLOYEES_TBL. You can enforce this logic by adding a foreign key on the EMPLOYEES_SALARY_TBL and setting it to point to the primary key of the EMPLOYEES_TBL. This will ensure that the data for each employee in the EMPLOYEES_SALARY_TBL are referenced to the specific employee listed in the EMPLOYEES_TBL. Consequently, it will also prevent the EMPLOYEES_SALARY table from storing data for names that are not included in the EMPLOYEES table.

To demonstrate how to set up the foreign key constraint, create a table named EMPLOYEE with the following statement:

```
mysql> CREATE TABLE EMPLOYEE(
    -> ID INT(4) NOT NULL,
    -> EMP_NAME CHAR(50) NOT NULL,
    -> ADDRESS VARCHAR(60) NOT NULL,
    -> PRIMARY KEY(ID)
    -> );
Query OK, 0 rows affected (0.81 sec)
```

The EMPLOYEE table will serve as the parent table.

Next, create a child table that will refer to the EMPLOYEES table:

```
mysql> CREATE TABLE EMPLOYEE_SALARY(
    -> ID INT(4) NOT NULL references EMPLOYEE(ID),
    -> Position VARCHAR(15) NOT NULL,
    -> Date_Hired DATE NOT NULL,
    -> SALARY DECIMAL(9,2),
    -> PRIMARY KEY(ID)
    -> );
Query OK, 0 rows affected (0.34 sec)
```

Notice that the ID column in the EMPLOYEE_SALARY TABLE references the ID column in the EMPLOYEE table.

At this point, you may want to see the structure of the EMPLOYEE_SALARY TABLE. You can use the DESC command to do this:

DESC EMPLOYEE_SALARY;

```
+---------------+---------------+------+-----+---------+-------+
| Field         | Type          | Null | Key | Default | Extra |
+---------------+---------------+------+-----+---------+-------+
| ID            | int(4)        | NO   | PRI | NULL    |       |
| Position      | varchar(15)   | NO   |     | NULL    |       |
| Date_Hired    | date          | NO   |     | NULL    |       |
| SALARY        | decimal(9,2)  | YES  |     | NULL    |       |
+---------------+---------------+------+-----+---------+-------+
4 rows in set (0.05 sec)
```

The FOREIGN KEY constraint is typically specified during table creation but you can still add a foreign key to existing tables by modifying the table. For this purpose, you will use the ALTER TABLE command.

For example, to add a foreign key constraint to the EMPLOYEE_SALARY table, you will use this statement:

ALTER TABLE EMPLOYEE_SALARY
ADD FOREIGN KEY(ID) INT NOT NULL REFERENCES EMPLOYEE(ID)

Removing FOREIGN KEY constraint

To drop a FOREIGN KEY constraint, you will use this simple syntax:

ALTER TABLE table_name
DROP FOREIGN KEY;

NOT NULL

A column contains NULL VALUES by default. To prevent NULL values from populating the table's column, you can implement a NOT NULL constraint on the column. Bear in mind that the word NULL pertains to unknown data and not zero data.

To illustrate, the following code creates the table STUDENTS and defines six columns:

```
CREATE TABLE STUDENTS (
    ID  INT  NOT NULL,
    LAST_NAME VARCHAR (30)  NOT NULL,
    FIRST_NAME VARCHAR (30)  NOT NULL,
    AGE INT   NOT NULL,
    LOCATION  CHAR (40) ,
    PRIMARY KEY (ID)
);
```

Notice the NOT NULL modifier on the columns ID, LAST_NAME, FIRST_NAME, and AGE. This means that these columns will not accept NULL values.

If you want to modify a column that takes a NULL value to one that does not accept NULL values, you can do so with the ALTER TABLE statement. For instance, if you want to enforce a NOT NULL constraint on the column LOCATION, here's the code:

```
ALTER TABLE STUDENTS
    MODIFY LOCATION CHAR (40) NOT NULL;
```

UNIQUE Key

A UNIQUE key constraint is used to ensure that all column values are unique. Enforcing this constraint prevents two or more rows from holding the same values in a particular column. For example, you can apply this constraint if you don't want two or more students to have the same LAST_NAME in the STUDENTS table. Here's the code:

```
CREATE TABLE STUDENTS (
    ID  INT  NOT NULL,
    NAME VARCHAR (50) NOT NULL UNIQUE,
    AGE INT    NOT NULL,
    LOCATION  CHAR (40) ,
    PRIMARY KEY (ID)
);
```

You can also use the ALTER TABLE statement to add a UNIQUE constraint to an existing table. Here's the code:

```
ALTER TABLE STUDENTS
    MODIFY NAME VARCHAR (50) NOT NULL UNIQUE;
```

You may also add constraint to more than one column by using ALTER TABLE with ADD CONSTRAINT:

```
ALTER TABLE STUDENTS
  ADD CONSTRAINT myUniqueConstraint UNIQUE(NAME, LOCATION);
```

Removing a UNIQUE constraint

To remove the myUniqueConstraint, you will use the ALTER TABLE with the DROP statement. Here's the syntax:

```
ALTER TABLE STUDENTS
    DROP CONSTRAINT myUniqueConstraint
```

DEFAULT Constraint

The DEFAULT constraint is used to provide a default value whenever the user fails to enter a value for a column during an INSERT INTO operation.

To demonstrate, the following code will create a table named EMPLOYEES with five columns. Notice that the SALARY column takes a default value (4000.00) which will be used if no value was provided when you add new records:

```
CREATE TABLE EMPLOYEES (
     ID  INT  NOT NULL,
     NAME (50)  NOT NULL,
     AGE INT    NOT NULL,
     LOCATION  CHAR (40) ,
     SALARY   DECIMAL(12, 2),  DEFAULT 4000.00,
     PRIMARY KEY (ID)
);
```

You may also use the ALTER STATEMENT to add a DEFAULT constraint to an existing table:

```
ALTER TABLE EMPLOYEES
  MODIFY SALARY DECIMAL(12,2) DEFAUL 4000.00;
```

Removing a Default Constraint

To remove a DEFAULT constraint, you will use the ALTER TABLE with the DROP statement:

```
ALTER TABLE EMPLOYEES
ALTER COLUMN SALARY DEFAULT;
```

CHECK Constraint

A CHECK constraint is used to ensure that each value entered in a column satisfies a given condition. An attempt to enter a non-matching data will result to a violation of the CHECK constraint which will cause the data to be rejected.

For example, the code below will create a table named GAMERS with five columns. It will place a CHECK constraint on the AGE column to ensure that there will be no gamers under 13 years old on the table.

```
CREATE TABLE GAMERS (
     ID  INT  NOT NULL,
     NAME (50)  NOT NULL,
     AGE  INT    NOT NULL, CHECK (AGE >= 13),
     LOCATION  CHAR (40) ,
     PRIMARY KEY (ID)
);
```

You can also use the ALTER TABLE statement with MODIFY to add the CHECK constraint to an existing table:

```
ALTER TABLE GAMERS
    MODIFY AGE INT NOT NULL CHECK(AGE>=13);
```

INDEX Constraint

The INDEX constraint lets you build and access information quickly from a database. You can easily create an index with one or more table columns. After the INDEX is created, SQL assigns a ROWID to each row prior to sorting. Proper indexing can enhance the performance and efficiency of large databases.

Here's the syntax:

```
CREATE INDEX index_name
    ON table_name(column1, column2, column3...);
```

For instance, if you need to search for a group of employees from a specific location in the EMPLOYEES table, you can create an INDEX on the column LOCATION.

Here's the code:

```
CREATE INDEX idx_loc
    ON EMPLOYEES(LOCATION);
```

Removing the INDEX Constraint

To remove the INDEX constraint, you will use the ALTER TABLE statement with DROP. Here's the code:

```
ALTER TABLE EMPLOYEES
    DROP INDEX idx_loc
```

Chapter 4: Database Creation

A database is a collection of data which is organized to be easily accessed and managed. Data is stored in tables and indexed to make queries more efficient. Before you can create tables, you need a database to hold the table. If you're starting from zero, you will have to learn to create and use a database.

Creating a Database

To create a database, you will use the command `CREATE` with the name of the database.

Syntax:

`CREATE DATABASE database_name;`

To demonstrate, assuming you want to create a database and name it as xyzcompany, you can use the following statement:

`CREATE DATABASE xyzcompany;`

With that statement, you have just created the xyzcompany database. Before you can use this database, you need to designate it as the active database. You have to run the USE command with the database name to activate your new database.

Here's the statement;

`USE xyzcompany;`

On succeeding sessions, you can just type the statement 'USE xyzcompany' to access the database.

Removing a Database

If you need to remove an existing database, you can easily do so with this syntax:

 DROP DATABASE databasename;

Bear in mind that you will lose all information stored in a database once it is deleted. Hence, you must exercise caution when using the DROP command to remove a database. You will also need admin privileges to drop a database.

Chapter 5: Schema Creation

The `CREATE SCHEMA` statement is used to define a schema. On the same statement, you can also create objects and grant privileges on these objects.

The `CREATE SCHEMA` command can be embedded within an application program. Likewise, it can be issued using dynamic SQL statements. For example, if you have database admin privileges, you can issue this statement which creates a schema called USER1 with the USER1 as its owner:

```
CREATE SCHEMA USER1 AUTHORIZATION USER1
```

The following statement creates a schema with an inventory table. It also grants authority on the inventory table to USER2:

CREATE SCHEMA INVENTORY

    CREATE TABLE ITEMS (IDNO INT(6) NOT NULL,
               SNAME   VARCHAR(40),
               CLASS INTEGER)

    GRANT ALL ON ITEMS TO USER2

The following section discusses the peculiarities of the CREATE SCHEMA statement among the different implementations of SQL.

MySQL 5.7

If you're using MySQL 5.7, CREATE SCHEMA is synonymous to the command CREATE DATABASE.

Here's the syntax:

```
CREATE {DATABASE | SCHEMA} [IF NOT EXISTS] db_name
  [create_specification] ...

create_specification:
  [DEFAULT] CHARACTER SET [=] charset_name
  | [DEFAULT] COLLATE [=] collation_name
```

Oracle 11g

In Oracle 11g, you can create several views and tables and perform several grants in one transaction within the CREATE SCHEMA statement. To successfully execute the CREATE SCHEMA command, Oracle runs each statement within the block and commits the transaction if no errors are encountered. If any statement returns an error, all statements are rolled back.

The statements CREATE VIEW, CREATE TABLE, and GRANT may be included within the CREATE SCHEMA statement. Hence, you must not only have the privilege to create a schema, you must also have the privileges needed to issue the statements within it.

Syntax:

```
CREATE SCHEMA AUTHORIZATION schema
  { create_table_statement
  | create_view_statement
  | grant_statement
  }...;
```

SQL Server 2014

In SQL Server 2014, the CREATE SCHEMA statement is used to create a schema in the current database. This transaction may also create views and tables within the newly-created schema and set GRANT, REVOKE, or DENY permission on these objects.

This statement creates a schema and sets the specifications for each argument:

CREATE SCHEMA schema_name_clause [<schema_element> [...n]]

```
<schema_name_clause> ::=
  {
  schema_name
  | AUTHORIZATION owner_name
  | schema_name AUTHORIZATION owner_name
  }

<schema_element> ::=
  {
     table_definition | view_definition | grant_statement |
     revoke_statement | deny_statement
  }
```

PostgreSQL 9.3.13

The CREATE SCHEMA statement is used to enter a new schema into a database. The schema name should be unique within the current database.

Here's the syntax:

```
CREATE SCHEMA schema_name [ AUTHORIZATION user_name ] [ schema_element [ ... ] ]
CREATE SCHEMA AUTHORIZATION user_name [ schema_element [ ... ] ]
CREATE SCHEMA IF NOT EXISTS schema_name [ AUTHORIZATION user_name ]
CREATE SCHEMA IF NOT EXISTS AUTHORIZATION user_name
```

Chapter 6: Creating Tables And Inserting Data Into Tables

Tables are the main storage of information in databases. Creating a table means specifying a name for a table, defining its columns, and the data type of each column. In this chapter, you will learn how to create tables and add data to tables.

How to Create a Table

The keyword CREATE TABLE is used to create a new table. It is followed by a unique identifier and a list that defines each column and the type of data it will hold.

This is the basic syntax for creating a table:

```
CREATE TABLE table_name
(
    column1 datatype [NULL | NOT NULL ],
    column2 datatype [NULL | NOT NULL ],
    ...
);
```

Parameters

table_name: This is the identifier for the table.

column1, column2: These are the columns that you want the table to have. All columns should have a data type. A column is defined as either NULL or NOT NULL. If this is not specified, the database will assume that it is NULL.

The following set of questions can serve as a guide when creating a new table:

- What is the most appropriate name for this table?
- What data types will I be working with?
- What is the most appropriate name for each column?
- Which column(s) should be used as the main key(s)?
- What type of data can be assigned to each column?
- What is the maximum width for each column?
- Which columns can be empty and which columns should not be empty?

The following example creates a new table with the xyzcompany database. It will be named EMPLOYEES:

```
CREATE TABLE EMPLOYEES(
ID INT(6) auto_increment, NOT NULL,
FIRST_NAME VARCHAR(35) NOT NULL,
LAST_NAME VARCHAR(35) NOT NULL,
POSITION VARCHAR(35),
SALARY DECIMAL(9,2).
ADDRESS VARCHAR(50),
PRIMARY KEY (id)
);
```

The code creates a table with 6 columns. The ID field was specified as its primary key. The first column is an INT data type with a precision of 6. It does not accept a NULL value. The second column, FIRST_NAME, is a VARCHAR type with a maximum range of 35 characters. The third column, LAST_NAME, is another VARCHAR type which takes a maximum of 35 characters. The fourth column, POSITION, is a VARCHAR type which is set at a maximum of 35 characters. The fifth column, SALARY, is a DECIMAL type with a precision of 9 and scale of 2. Finally, the fifth column, ADDRESS, is a VARCHAR type with a maximum of 50 characters. The id column was designated as the primary key.

Creating New Table from Existing Tables

You can create a new table based on an existing table by using the CREATE TABLE keyword with SELECT.

Here's the syntax:

```
CREATE TABLE new_table_name AS
(
    SELECT [column1, column, 2...columnN]
    FROM existing_table_name
    [WHERE]
);
```

Executing this code will create a new table with column definitions that are identical to the original table. You may copy all columns or select specific columns for the new table. The new table will be populated by the values of the original table.

To demonstrate, create a duplicate table named STOCKHOLDERS from the existing table EMPLOYEES within the xyzcomppany. The new table will have the same column names and definitions. Here's the code:

```
CREATE TABLE STOCKHOLDERS AS
SELECT ID, FIRST_NAME, LAST_NAME, POSITION,
SALARY, ADDRESS
FROM EMPLOYEES;
```

Inserting Data into Table

SQL's Data Manipulation Language (DML) is used to perform changes to databases. You can use DML clauses to fill a table with fresh data, update an existing table, and remove data that you no longer need.

Populating a Table with New Data

There are two ways to fill a table with new information: manual entry or automated entry through a computer program.

Populating data manually involves data entry using a keyboard. Automated entry involves loading data from an external source. It may include transferring data from one database to a target database.

Unlike SQL keywords or clauses which are case-insensitive, data is case-sensitive. Hence, you have to ensure consistency when using or referring to data. For instance, if you store an employee's first name as 'Martin', succeeding usage or references to the name should be 'Martin' and never 'MARTIN' or 'martin'.

The `INSERT` Keyword

The `INSERT` keyword is used to add records to a table. It inserts new rows of data to an existing table.

There are two ways to add data with the `INSERT` keyword. In the first format, you will simply provide the values for each field and they will be assigned sequentially to the table's columns. This form is generally used if you need to add data to all columns.

You will use this syntax for the first form:

```
INSERT INTO table_name
VALUES ('value1', 'value2', [NULL];
```

In the second form, you'll have to include the column names. The values will be assigned based on the order of the columns' appearance. This form is typically used if you want to add records to specific columns.

Here's the syntax:

```
INSERT INTO table_name (column1, column2, column3)
VALUES ('value1', 'value2', 'value3');
```

Notice that in both forms, a comma is used to separate the columns and the values. In addition, you have to enclose character/string and date/time data within quotation marks.

Assuming that you have the following record for an employee:

First Name   Robert
Last Name   Page
Position   Clerk
Salary   5,000.00
282 Patterson Avenue Illinois

To insert this data into the EMPLOYEES table, you can use the following statement:

```
INSERT     INTO     EMPLOYEES     (FIRST_NAME,
LAST_NAME, POSITION, SALARY, ADDRESS)
VALUES ('Robert', 'Page', 'Clerk', 5000.00,
'282 Patterson Avenue, Illinois');
```

To view the updated table, here's the syntax:

```
SELECT * FROM table_name;
```

To display the data stored in the EMPLOYEES' table, you will use this statement:

SELECT * FROM EMPLOYEES;

The wildcard (*) character tells the database system to select all fields on the table.

Here's a screenshot of the result:

```
mysql> SELECT * FROM EMPLOYEES;
+----+------------+-----------+----------+---------+---------------------------------
----+
| ID | FIRST_NAME | LAST_NAME | POSITION | SALARY  | ADDRESS
    |
+----+------------+-----------+----------+---------+---------------------------------
----+
|  1 | Robert     | Page      | Clerk    | 5000.00 | 282 Patterson Avenue, Illin
ois |
+----+------------+-----------+----------+---------+---------------------------------
----+
```

Now, try to encode the following data for another set of employees:

First Name	Last Name	Position	Salary	Address
John	Malley	Supervisor	7,000.00	5 Lake View, New York
Kristen	Johnston	Clerk	4,500.00	25 Jump Road, Florida
Jack	Burns	Agent	5,000.00	5 Green Meadows, California

You will have to repeatedly use the INSERT INTO keyword to enter each employee data to the database. Here's how the statements would look:

```
INSERT INTO EMPLOYEES(FIRST_NAME, LAST_NAME,
POSITION, SALARY, ADDRESS)
VALUES('John',    'Malley',    'Supervisor',
7000.00, '5 Lake View New York);
```

```
INSERT INTO EMPLOYEES(FIRST_NAME, LAST_NAME,
POSITION, SALARY, ADDRESS)
VALUES('Kristen',      'Johnston',      'Clerk',
4000.00, '25  Jump Road, Florida');

INSERT INTO EMPLOYEES(FIRST_NAME, LAST_NAME,
POSITION, SALARY, ADDRESS)
VALUES('Jack', 'Burns', 'Agent', 5000.00, '5
Green Meadows, California')';
```

To fetch the updated EMPLOYEES table, use the `SELECT` command with the wild card character.

SELECT * FROM EMPLOYEES;

Here's a screenshot of the result:

```
mysql> SELECT * FROM EMPLOYEES;
+----+------------+-----------+------------+---------+---------------------------
------+
| ID | FIRST_NAME | LAST_NAME | POSITION   | SALARY  | ADDRESS
    |
+----+------------+-----------+------------+---------+---------------------------
------+
|  1 | Robert     | Page      | Clerk      | 5000.00 | 282 Patterson Avenue, Ill
inois |
|  2 | John       | Malley    | Supervisor | 7000.00 | 5 Lake View New York
    |
|  3 | Kristen    | Johnston  | Clerk      | 4000.00 | 25 Jump Road Florida
    |
|  4 | Jack       | Burns     | Agent      | 5000.00 | 5 Green Meadows Californi
a     |
+----+------------+-----------+------------+---------+---------------------------
------+
4 rows in set (0.00 sec)
```

Notice that SQL assigned an ID number for each set of data you entered. This is because you have defined the ID column with the auto_increment attribute. This property will prevent you from using the first form when inserting data. That is, you have to specify the rest of the columns in the INSERT INTO table_name line.

Inserting Data into Specific Columns

You may also insert data into specific column(s). You can do this by specifying the column name inside the column list and the corresponding values inside the VALUES list of the INSERT INTO statement. For example, if you only want to enter an employee's full name and position, you will need to specify the column names FIRST_NAME, LAST_NAME, and SALARY in the columns list and the values for the first name, last name, and salary inside the VALUES list.

To see how this works, try entering the following data into the EMPLOYEES table:

First Name	Last Name	Position	Salary	Address
James	Hunt		7,500.00	

Here's a screenshot of the updated EMPLOYEES table:

```
+----+------------+-----------+------------+----------+------------------------------+
| ID | FIRST_NAME | LAST_NAME | POSITION   | SALARY   | ADDRESS                      |
+----+------------+-----------+------------+----------+------------------------------+
|  1 | Robert     | Page      | Clerk      | 5000.00  | 282 Patterson Avenue, Illinois |
|  2 | John       | Malley    | Supervisor | 7000.00  | 5 Lake View New York         |
|  3 | Kristen    | Johnston  | Clerk      | 4000.00  | 25 Jump Road Florida         |
|  4 | Jack       | Burns     | Agent      | 5000.00  | 5 Green Meadows California    |
|  5 | James      | Hunt      | NULL       | 7500.00  | NULL                         |
+----+------------+-----------+------------+----------+------------------------------+
5 rows in set (0.00 sec)
```

Inserting NULL Values

In some instances, you may have to enter NULL values into a column. For example, you may not have data on hand to enter a new employee's salary. It may be misleading to provide just about any salary figure. In such cases, it may be better to simply enter the keyword NULL into the SALARY column.

Here's the syntax:

```
INSERT INTO schema.table_name
VALUES ('column1', NULL, 'column3');
```

Chapter 7: Data Manipulation

Sql Statements

The Data Manipulation Language (DML) of SQL contains the list of commands that you can use to manipulate and work with data within tables. They include the following statements:

SELECT   This statement is used to retrieve data from the table.

INSERT   This is used to insert data into a table.

UPDATE   The UPDATE statement updates existing table data.

DELETE   This statement deletes records from a table but maintains the space they occupy.

These statements will be discussed lengthily in the following sections.

Apart from these statements, some statements are also used to control the transaction made by DML statements. The commands used for this purpose are called Transaction Control (TCL) statements. These allow statements to be grouped into logical transactions. Some commands include:

COMMIT
This command is used to save the word done permanently.

SAVEPOINT
This statement identifies a point in a transaction which you can use to roll back to later.

ROLLBACK

This command is used to restore the database to its original status since the last COMMIT transaction.

Selecting Data

The Data Query Language (DQL) is considered as the most powerful aspect of SQL. This group consists of a single command: SELECT.

The SELECT command is commonly used to run queries for relational databases. It can be used with other clauses to obtain more detailed and relevant results.

Earlier, you have learned that the SELECT command can be used to return a set of data stored on a table. In this chapter, you will learn how to use it to retrieve any data you may need through database queries.

Queries are inquiries made into a database using the SELECT command. This command is used to search for and display the data stored within a database. For example, if a database contains a table that stores sales information, you can launch a query to determine your company's bestselling product. Modern relational databases provide highly useful information through queries.

The SELECT Command

The SELECT Command is used to start and perform queries on a database. It is commonly used with other SQL clauses to launch a query. Some of these clauses are mandatory while some are optional. They are used to improve the effectiveness of database queries.

The SELECT clause is used to select the data that you want to fetch from the database. It is used to indicate the column or list of columns that will be used as the basis for the search.

The FROM keyword

The FROM keyword is an integral part of any database query. It is combined with the SELECT command to obtain the desired data in an organized format. You will use it to identify the table(s) that you want to access during the search. You will need to specify at least one table as the source of your query. It is a mandatory element of a query.

A basic query will have this syntax:

SELECT column1, column2, column3 FROM table_name;

To demonstrate, assume that you want to launch a query on the EMPLOYEES table to extract information for the columns LAST_NAME, FIRST_NAME, and SALARY. Here's what the statement would be:

```
SELECT LAST_NAME, FIRST_NAME, SALARY FROM
EMPLOYEES;
```

Here's the result:

```
+-----------+------------+---------+
| LAST_NAME | FIRST_NAME | SALARY  |
+-----------+------------+---------+
| Page      | Robert     | 5000.00 |
| Malley    | John       | 7000.00 |
| Johnston  | Kristen    | 4000.00 |
| Hunt      | James      | 7500.00 |
+-----------+------------+---------+
4 rows in set (0.00 sec)
```

Limiting the Rows of Data to be Displayed

If you're running a large database with tables that contain thousands of rows, you query may also output thousand of results which may consume your resources and slow down the query. In such situations, you may need to limit the number of rows that will be returned in the result set. SQL provides the LIMIT clause which lets you define the number of rows that the query will display.

For example, this statement will limit the display of data to only three rows for a query made in the EMPLOYEES table:

```
SELECT LAST_NAME, FIRST_NAME, SALARY FROM
EMPLOYEES
LIMIT 3;
```

The statement will produce the following result:

```
+------------+------------+----------+
| LAST_NAME  | FIRST_NAME | SALARY   |
+------------+------------+----------+
| Page       | Robert     | 5000.00  |
| Malley     | John       | 7000.00  |
| Johnston   | Kristen    | 4000.00  |
+------------+------------+----------+
3 rows in set (0.63 sec)
```

Updating Data

The UPDATE command is used to modify or update data in a table. You may use it to change one or more rows. Take note that it is only used to modify an existing table. You cannot use it to add or remove data on a table. It is typically used with the WHERE clause to limit its application to records that meet the criteria.

Here's the syntax:

```
UPDATE table_name
SET column1=value1, column2=value2
WHERE some_column=value;
```

In SQL update statements, the UPDATE keyword specifies the name of the table that will be updated. The SET keyword indicates what column(s) will be updated. The WHERE keyword defines the condition(s) and limits the record(s) that will be affected by the statement. Omitting the WHERE clause will cause all records to be updated.

For example, assuming that you have to update Kristen Johnston's salary to $7,000, here's what the code might be:

```
UPDATE EMPLOYEES
SET SALARY=7000.00
WHERE LAST_NAME='Johnston';
```

Filtering Data

WHERE

The WHERE keyword is used to specify one or more conditions to refine the query. If the specified condition is met, it will return the selected values. You can use it when fetching information from a table or when joining with multiple tables. This clause is used to filter table data and display only the records that you need.

While it is more frequently used with the SELECT command, the WHERE clause is also used with other SQL commands such as DELETE or UPDATE.

You can specify one or more conditions to further refine your query. If you're using more than one condition, you will have to connect them with SQL operators such as OR, AND, =, <, >, and LIKE.

Here's the syntax for SELECT command with a WHERE clause:

```
SELECT column1, column2, column3
FROM table_name
WHERE [condition];
```

To demonstrate, you can filter the EMPLOYEES table to display the first name and last name of employees with a salary higher than 5,000. Here's the statement:

```
SELECT LAST_NAME, FIRST_NAME FROM EMPLOYEES
WHERE SALARY >5000.00;
```

Here's the result:

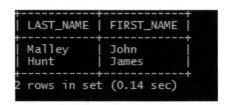

Ordering Data

ORDER BY

This clause is used if you want to sort the output of a query in ascending or descending order. When no sorting order is defined, it sorts the results data in an ascending order. Hence, if you're working with character or text types, the result will be displayed from A-Z by default.

Here's the syntax:

```
SELECT columN1, column2
FROM table_name
[WHERE condition]
[ORDER BY column2, column2] [ASC | DESC];
```

For example, this statement will sort the EMPLOYEES table in an ascending order based on last name and salary:

```
SELECT * FROM EMPLOYEES
    ORDER BY LAST_NAME, SALARY ASC;
```

Here's the result :

```
+------+------------+-----------+------------+---------+--------------------------+
| ID  | FIRST_NAME | LAST_NAME | POSITION   | SALARY  | ADDRESS                  |
+------+------------+-----------+------------+---------+--------------------------+
|   5 | James      | Hunt      | NULL       | 7500.00 | NULL                     |
|   3 | Kristen    | Johnston  | Clerk      | 4000.00 | 25 Jump Road Florida     |
|   2 | John       | Malley    | Supervisor | 7000.00 | 5 Lake View New York     |
|   1 | Robert     | Page      | Clerk      | 5000.00 | 282 Patterson Avenue, Illinois |
+------+------------+-----------+------------+---------+--------------------------+
4 rows in set (0.23 sec)
```

This statement will sort the result in a descending order:

```
SELECT * FROM EMPLOYEES
    ORDER BY LAST_NAME, SALARY DESC;
```

Here's the output:

```
------+
| ID | FIRST_NAME | LAST_NAME | POSITION   | SALARY  | ADDRESS
      |
+----+------------+-----------+------------+---------+----------------------------
------+
| 5 | James       | Hunt      | NULL       | 7500.00 | NULL
      |
| 3 | Kristen     | Johnston  | Clerk      | 4000.00 | 25 Jump Road Florida
      |
| 2 | John        | Malley    | Supervisor | 7000.00 | 5 Lake View New York
      |
| 1 | Robert      | Page      | Clerk      | 5000.00 | 282 Patterson Avenue, Ill
inois |
+----+------------+-----------+------------+---------+----------------------------
------+
4 rows in set (0.00 sec)
```

Grouping Data

The GROUP BY clause in a SELECT statement lets you arrange the result-set based on a single or multiple columns. It is frequently used with aggregate functions such as SUM, COUNT, AVG, MAX, and MIN.

The GROUP BY clause must be placed before the ORDER BY clause and after the WHERE clause.

The following is a basic syntax for this clause:

SELECT column_name(s)
FROM table_name
WHERE condition
GROUP BY column_name(s)
ORDER BY column_name(s);

The examples in this section will use the following table named Store_Sales:

Branch	Product_ID	Sales	Region
New York City	101	7500.00	East
Los Angeles	102	6450.00	West
Chicago	101	1560.00	East
Philadelphia	101	1980.00	East

Denver	102	3500.00	West
Seattle	101	2500.00	West
Detroit	102	1450.00	East

There are several ways to group the data in this table. If you want to find the total sales per region, you can use this statement:

```
SELECT Region, SUM(Sales)
FROM Store_Sales
GROUP BY Region;
```

This would be the result:

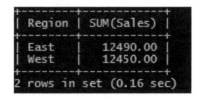

Assuming you want to find the total sales per product, here's the statement:

SELECT PRODUCT_ID, SUM(Sales)
FROM Store_Sales
GROUP BY PRODUCT_ID;

Here's the result:

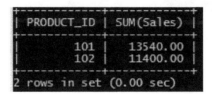

You can also use GROUP BY with multiple columns. For example, you may want to know the total sales per product at each region. You can use this statement:

SELECT Region, Product_ID, SUM(Sales)
FROM Store_Sales
GROUP BY Region, Product_ID;

The output would be:

```
+----------+------------+------------+
| Region   | Product_ID | SUM(Sales) |
+----------+------------+------------+
| East     |        101 |   11040.00 |
| East     |        102 |    1450.00 |
| West     |        101 |    2500.00 |
| West     |        102 |    9950.00 |
+----------+------------+------------+
4 rows in set (0.00 sec)
```

In addition, you can use GROUP BY with multiple functions. For instance, you may want to find both total sales and average sales for each product per region. To get that result, you can enter this statement:

SELECT Region, Product_ID, SUM(Sales), AVG(Sales)
FROM Store_Sales
GROUP BY Region, Product_ID;

This would be the result:

```
+----------+------------+------------+-------------+
| Region   | Product_ID | SUM(Sales) | AVG(Sales)  |
+----------+------------+------------+-------------+
| East     |        101 |   11040.00 | 3680.000000 |
| East     |        102 |    1450.00 | 1450.000000 |
| West     |        101 |    2500.00 | 2500.000000 |
| West     |        102 |    9950.00 | 4975.000000 |
+----------+------------+------------+-------------+
4 rows in set (0.03 sec)
```

Like and Wildcards

The LIKE is a logical operator that you can use in conjunction with wildcards to perform pattern comparison in a query. You can use it inside the WHERE clause of a SELECT, UPDATE, DELETE, or INSERT statement.

You can use the LIKE operator with two wildcards:

percent sign: %   This represents one, zero, or several characters.

underscore: _   This represents a character or number.

You may combine the percent and underscore operators in a single clause. In addition, you can specify more than one condition using the AND or OR operators.

To give you a better idea of its usage, here are examples of WHERE clauses with the LIKE operator:

WHERE First_Name LIKE 'A%	Finds values that begin with "A"
WHERE Name LIKE '%me%'	Finds values with "me" in any position
WHERE CustName LIKE '_o%'	Finds values with "o" in the second position
WHERE CustName LIKE 'D_%_%'	Finds values that begin with 'D' and have a minimum of 3 characters
WHERE EmpName LIKE 'B%K'	Finds values that begin with "B" and ends with "K"
WHERE SALARY LIKE '3000%'	Searches for values that begin with 3000.
WHERE SALARY LIKE '%500%'	Searches for values with 500 in any position.

WHERE SALARY LIKE '_oo%'	Searches for values with oo in the second and third positions
WHERE SALARY LIKE '4_%_%'	Finds values that start with 4 and are at least 3 characters in length.
WHERE POSITION LIKE 'F%'	Finds values that begin with "F"
WHERE CustomerName LIKE '%a'	Finds values that end with "a"
WHERE CustomerName LIKE '%or%'	Finds values that have "or" in any position
WHERE CustomerName LIKE '_r%'	Finds values that have "r" in the second position
WHERE CustomerName LIKE 'R_%_%'	Finds values that begin with "R" and have a minimum of 3 characters
WHERE ContactName LIKE 'J%o'	Finds values that begin with "J" and ends with "o"

If you are using char data type for pattern matching, remember that chars are padded with spaces at the end to fill the length of the field. This may give you unexpected results when you use the LIKE condition to match patterns at the end of a string.

Subqueries

A subquery is a query nested within an SQL query and embedded inside a WHERE, FROM, or SELECT clause. It is also called a Nested query, Inner Select, or Inner query. You will typically use a subquery to fetch data needed in the main query. A subquery executes ahead of the main query so that its result can be passed to it. You may use comparison operators such as <. >,=, or multiple row operators like ANY, BETWEEN, ALL, or IN.

You can use subqueries with the SELECT, UPDATE, INSERT, or DELETE statements to perform these tasks:

- Compare the result of the query to an expression.
- Ascertain if a given expression can be found in the query results.
- Verify if the query selects a row.

When using subqueries, you must take note of the following rules:

- Subqueries should be placed inside parentheses.

- A subquery cannot use an ORDER BY clause because it can't manipulate its result internally. You may only use it in the SELECT statement of the outer query as the last clause. Subqueries may use the GROUP BY clause in its place to perform the same functions.

- Subqueries can only take a single column in a SELECT clause except when it requires multiple selected columns for comparison with the multiple columns in the main query.

- A subquery can't be directly enclosed in a set function.

- The SELECT list should not include references to values that result to an ARRAY, BLOB, NCLOB, or CLOB.

- A subquery that returns multiple rows requires multiple value operators. Single-row subqueries require single-row operators.

- Subqueries are written on the right side of comparison operators.

A subquery can return a single row, multiple rows, or multiple columns. They can be nested or correlated.

Subquery with SELECT Statement

Subqueries are most commonly used with the SELECT statement.

Here's the basic syntax:

```
SELECT column_name [, column_name ]
FROM   table1 [, table2 ]
WHERE  column_name OPERATOR
  (SELECT column_name [, column_name ]
  FROM table1 [, table2 ]
  [WHERE])
```

To demonstrate, you will use the following table:

SALES_REP TABLE

ID	EMP_NAME	SALES	BRANCH
1001	ALAN MARSCH	1,500.00	NEW YORK
2005	RAIN ALONZO	2,000.00	NEW YORK
3008	MARK FIELDING	3,555.00	CHICAGO
4810	MAINE ROD	3,500.00	NEW YORK
5783	JACK RINGER	6,000.00	CHICAGO
6431	MARK TWAIN	5,000.00	LOS ANGELES
7543	JACKIE FELTS	3,500.00	CHICAGO
8934	MARK GOTH	5,400.00	AUSTIN
9876	JANINE SAINTS	2,100.00	AUSTIN
1098	NEIL BANKS	2,700.00	LOS ANGELES
2876	RYAN ALMS	5,700.00	NEW YORK
4356	JENNER BANKS	7,300.00	NEW YORK

The objective of this subquery is to produce a report that will show the names and branch of employees with sales of more than 3,000.00. Here's the statement:

```
SQL> SELECT EMP_NAME, BRANCH FROM SALES _REP
    WHERE ID IN (SELECT ID FROM SALES
        WHERE SALES > 3000.00);
```

This is the output of the subquery:

```
+----------------+---------------+
| EMP_NAME       | BRANCH        |
+----------------+---------------+
| MARK FIELDING  | CHICAGO       |
| JENNER BANKS   | NEW YORK      |
| MAINE ROD      | NEW YORK      |
| JACK RINGER    | CHICAGO       |
| MARK TWAIN     | LOS ANGELES   |
| JACKIE FELTS   | CHICAGO       |
| MARK GOTH      | AUSTIN        |
+----------------+---------------+
7 rows in set (0.45 sec)
```

Subquery with the INSERT Statement

You may also use subqueries with INSERT statements. Data returned from a subquery can be inserted into a table. The selected data may be modified using date, number, or character functions.

Here's the syntax:

```
INSERT INTO table_name [ (column1 [, column2 ]) ]
  SELECT [ *|column1 [, column2 ]
  FROM table1 [, table2 ]
  [ WHERE VALUE OPERATOR ]
```

To illustrate, assume that a table named SALES_DATA has the same structure as the SALES table. You can copy the entire SALES_REP table into the SALES_DATA table using the following syntax:

```
INSERT INTO SALES_DATA
    SELECT * FROM SALES_REP
    WHERE ID IN (SELECT ID
    FROM SALES_REP);
```

You now have two tables with identical structures and data.

Subquery with the UPDATE Statement

Likewise, you may use subqueries with the UPDATE statement. The use of a subquery with the UPDATE statement results in the updating of one or more columns in a table.

Here's the basic syntax:

```
UPDATE table
SET column_name = new_value
[ WHERE OPERATOR [ VALUE ]
  (SELECT COLUMN_NAME
  FROM TABLE_NAME)
  [ WHERE) ]
```

The following example updates the SALES by 2x in the SALES_REP table for all employees whose BRANCH is equal to Los Angeles:

```
UPDATE SALES_REP
    SET SALES = SALES * 2
    WHERE BRANCH IN (SELECT BRANCH FROM
SALES_REP
        WHERE BRANCH = 'LOS ANGELES');
```

Here's the updated SALES table:

```
+-------+-----------------+-----------+---------------+
| ID    | EMP_NAME        | SALES     | BRANCH        |
+-------+-----------------+-----------+---------------+
| 1001  | ALAN MARSCH     | 3000.00   | NEW YORK      |
| 1098  | NEIL BANKS      | 5400.00   | LOS ANGELES   |
| 2005  | RAIN ALONZO     | 4000.00   | NEW YORK      |
| 3008  | MARK FIELDING   | 3555.00   | CHICAGO       |
| 4356  | JENNER BANKS    | 14600.00  | NEW YORK      |
| 4810  | MAINE ROD       | 7000.00   | NEW YORK      |
| 5783  | JACK RINGER     | 6000.00   | CHICAGO       |
| 6431  | MARK TWAIN      | 10000.00  | LOS ANGELES   |
| 7543  | JACKIE FELTS    | 3500.00   | CHICAGO       |
| 8934  | MARK GOTH       | 5400.00   | AUSTIN        |
| 9876  | JANINE SAINTS   | 2100.00   | AUSTIN        |
+-------+-----------------+-----------+---------------+
11 rows in set (0.00 sec)
```

Notice that the statement updated the SALES field for the two Los Angeles Branch employees: Neil Banks and Mark Twain.

Subquery with the DELETE Statement

You can also perform subqueries with the delete statement.

Here's the syntax:

```
DELETE FROM TABLE_NAME
[ WHERE OPERATOR [ VALUE ]
   (SELECT COLUMN_NAME
   FROM TABLE_NAME)
   [ WHERE) ]
```

For example, assuming that you have a backup file of the SALES_REP table named SALES_DATA, the following code will delete records from the SALES_REP table for all employees with sales that are less than 2500.00:

```
DELETE FROM SALES_REP
   WHERE SALES IN (SELECT SALES FROM
SALES_DATA
      WHERE SALES < = 2500.00);
```

The code will delete the record of the employee whose sales is less than 2500.00: Janine Saints.

Here's what the output would be:

```
+-------+---------------+----------+-------------+
| ID    | EMP_NAME      | SALES    | BRANCH      |
+-------+---------------+----------+-------------+
| 1001  | ALAN MARSCH   |  3000.00 | NEW YORK    |
| 1098  | NEIL BANKS    |  5400.00 | LOS ANGELES |
| 2005  | RAIN ALONZO   |  4000.00 | NEW YORK    |
| 3008  | MARK FIELDING |  3555.00 | CHICAGO     |
| 4356  | JENNER BANKS  | 14600.00 | NEW YORK    |
| 4810  | MAINE ROD     |  7000.00 | NEW YORK    |
| 5783  | JACK RINGER   |  6000.00 | CHICAGO     |
| 6431  | MARK TWAIN    | 10000.00 | LOS ANGELES |
| 7543  | JACKIE FELTS  |  3500.00 | CHICAGO     |
| 8934  | MARK GOTH     |  5400.00 | AUSTIN      |
+-------+---------------+----------+-------------+
10 rows in set (0.00 sec)
```

NULL Value

In SQL, the word NULL represents a missing value. When a field has a NULL value, it means that it has no value. A field with a NULL value is not the same as a field with zero value or one that contains spaces.

When a field is optional or was not declared with the NOT NULL constraint, you may or may not add a value to it when you're inserting or updating a record. By default, SQL saves the field with a NULL value.

Testing for NULL Values

The operators IS NULL and IS NOT NULL are used to test for NULL values in a table.

Syntax:

```
IS NULL
```

SELECT column_names
FROM table_name
WHERE column_name IS NULL;

```
IS NOT NULL
```

SELECT column_names
FROM table_name
WHERE column_name IS NOT NULL;

To demonstrate, you will be using the EMPLOYEES table with the following data:

```
+----+------------+-----------+------------+---------+------------------------------
| ID | FIRST_NAME | LAST_NAME | POSITION   | SALARY  | ADDRESS
+----+------------+-----------+------------+---------+------------------------------
|  1 | Robert     | Page      | Clerk      | 5000.00 | 282 Patterson Avenue, Ill
inois |
|  2 | John       | Malley    | Supervisor | 7000.00 | 5 Lake View New York
|  3 | Kristen    | Johnston  | Clerk      | 4000.00 | 25 Jump Road Florida
|  5 | James      | Hunt      | NULL       | 7500.00 | NULL
+----+------------+-----------+------------+---------+------------------------------
4 rows in set (0.02 sec)
```

The statement below will use the IS NULL operator to list all employees without address:

```
SELECT LAST_NAME, FIRST_NAME, ADDRESS FROM
EMPLOYEES
WHERE ADDRESS IS NULL;
```

This would be the output:

```
+------------+-------------+----------+
| LAST_NAME  | FIRST_NAME  | ADDRESS  |
+------------+-------------+----------+
| Hunt       | James       | NULL     |
+------------+-------------+----------+
1 row in set (0.93 sec)
```

This statement will use the IS NOT NULL operator to list employees with address:

```
SELECT LAST_NAME, FIRST_NAME, ADDRESS FROM
EMPLOYEES
WHERE ADDRESS IS NOT NULL;
```

Here's the result:

```
+------------+-------------+-------------------------------------+
| LAST_NAME  | FIRST_NAME  | ADDRESS                             |
+------------+-------------+-------------------------------------+
| Page       | Robert      | 282 Patterson Avenue, Illinois      |
| Malley     | John        | 5 Lake View New York                |
| Johnston   | Kristen     | 25 Jump Road Florida                |
+------------+-------------+-------------------------------------+
3 rows in set (0.03 sec)
```

Deleting Data

The DELETE statement is used to remove rows of data from a table. The DELETE statement will eliminate an entire row of data so you need to be extremely careful when you use it.

Here's the syntax for the DELETE statement:

```
DELETE FROM table_name
WHERE some_column=somevalue;
```

The DELETE statement uses the WHERE clause to specify the record(s) that will be deleted. If you omit this clause, the DELETE command will delete all of your records. Keep in mind that the inadvertent use of this statement can potentially inflict permanent damage to your database.

Ideally, you may be able to undo an erroneous deletion by restoring a recent back up. If the backup isn't updated, it may not be possible to retrieve the data prior to the deletion. You may have to manually re-enter the original date. Although it will probably not mean a lot of work for databases with a few rows, manual encoding can take a longer time if you have to deal with thousands of records.

To illustrate, you can delete all records pertaining to the employee Jack Burns in the EMPLOYEES table with this statement:

```
DELETE FROM EMPLOYEES
WHERE LAST_NAME = 'Burns';
```

Here's what's left of the EMPLOYEES table after deleting one row:

```
+----+------------+------------+------------+----------+-----------------------------+
| ID | FIRST_NAME | LAST_NAME  | POSITION   | SALARY   | ADDRESS                     |
+----+------------+------------+------------+----------+-----------------------------+
|  1 | Robert     | Page       | Clerk      | 5000.00  | 282 Patterson Avenue, Illinois |
|  2 | John       | Malley     | Supervisor | 7000.00  | 5 Lake View New York        |
|  3 | Kristen    | Johnston   | Clerk      | 4000.00  | 25 Jump Road Florida        |
|  5 | James      | Hunt       | NULL       | 7500.00  | NULL                        |
+----+------------+------------+------------+----------+-----------------------------+
4 rows in set (0.00 sec)
```

Deleting all Data

By omitting the WHERE clause, you can use the DELETE statement to remove the entire rows of a table without actually removing the table. In such cases, the table will retain its attributes, structures, and indices.

Here are possible statements to delete all data without deleting the table:

63

DELETE FROM table_name

DELETE * FROM table_name

Chapter 8: SQL Operators

An operator is a special character or word that defines a condition or links one or more conditions in an SQL statement. Operators are primarily used in the WHERE clause. SQL supports a wide range of operators for performing arithmetic, comparison, or logical operations.

SQL Arithmetic Operators

SQL supports the following arithmetic operators:

+	Addition - Adds left and right operands
-	Subtraction - Subtracts right hand operand from left hand operand
*	Multiplication - Multiplies the left and right operands
/	Division - Divides left hand operand by right hand operand
%	Modulus - Divides left hand operand by right hand operand and returns remainder

In this section, you will learn how you can use arithmetic operators to obtain the information you may need from a database.

Addition (+)

This statement uses the addition operator to add the values of the columns RAW_MATERIALS and OVERHEAD from a table named PRODUCTION_COST:

```
SELECT RAW_MATERIALS + OVERHEAD FROM PRODUCTION_COST_TBL
```

Subtraction (-)

The following statement deducts the value of the column DIRECT_COST from the value of the column SALES based on data stored in FINANCIALS table:

```
SELECT SALES - DIRECT_COST FROM FINANCIALS_TBL
```

Multiplication (*)

The asterisk (*) is used to perform multiplication in SQL. In this example, the value of the SALES column from a table named FINANCIALS will be multiplied by 6:

```
SELECT SALES * 6 FROM FINANCIALS_TBL
```

Division (/)

The slash symbol is used to perform division in SQL. In the following statement, the
value of the SALES column from the FINANCIALS table will be divided by 12:

```
SELECT SALES / 12 FROM FINANCIALS_TBL
```

SQL Comparison Operators

Comparison operators are used to compare the values of two operands. SQL supports the following comparison operators:

Operator	Description
=	Checks if the left and right operands are equal
!=	Checks if the left and right operands are not equal
<>	Checks of the left and right operands are equal or not equal
>	Checks if the left operand is greater than the right operand
<	Checks if the left operand is less than the right operand
>=	Checks if the left operand is greater than or equal to the right operand
<=	Checks if the left operand is less than or equal to the right operand
!<	Checks if the left operand is not less than the right operand
!>	Checks if the left operand is not greater than the right operand

The examples in this section will use the SALES_REP table with the following data:

```
+-------+---------------+-----------+-------------+
| ID    | EMP_NAME      | SALES     | BRANCH      |
+-------+---------------+-----------+-------------+
| 1001  | ALAN MARSCH   | 3000.00   | NEW YORK    |
| 1098  | NEIL BANKS    | 5400.00   | LOS ANGELES |
| 2005  | RAIN ALONZO   | 4000.00   | NEW YORK    |
| 3008  | MARK FIELDING | 3555.00   | CHICAGO     |
| 4356  | JENNER BANKS  | 14600.00  | NEW YORK    |
| 4810  | MAINE ROD     | 7000.00   | NEW YORK    |
| 5783  | JACK RINGER   | 6000.00   | CHICAGO     |
| 6431  | MARK TWAIN    | 10000.00  | LOS ANGELES |
| 7543  | JACKIE FELTS  | 3500.00   | CHICAGO     |
| 8934  | MARK GOTH     | 5400.00   | AUSTIN      |
+-------+---------------+-----------+-------------+
10 rows in set (0.00 sec)
```

Here are some statements that you may use to extract data from the SALES_REP table:

```
SELECT * FROM SALES_REP WHERE SALES < 4000;
```

Output:

```
+------+------------------+----------+----------+
| ID   | EMP_NAME         | SALES    | BRANCH   |
+------+------------------+----------+----------+
| 1001 | ALAN MARSCH      | 3000.00  | NEW YORK |
| 3008 | MARK FIELDING    | 3555.00  | CHICAGO  |
| 7543 | JACKIE FELTS     | 3500.00  | CHICAGO  |
+------+------------------+----------+----------+
3 rows in set (0.07 sec)
```

SELECT * FROM SALES_REP WHERE SALES >= 7000.00;

Output:

```
+------+---------------+----------+-------------+
| ID   | EMP_NAME      | SALES    | BRANCH      |
+------+---------------+----------+-------------+
| 4356 | JENNER BANKS  | 14600.00 | NEW YORK    |
| 4810 | MAINE ROD     | 7000.00  | NEW YORK    |
| 6431 | MARK TWAIN    | 10000.00 | LOS ANGELES |
+------+---------------+----------+-------------+
3 rows in set (0.00 sec)
```

SQL Logical Operators

ALL	Compares a value to all values of a different set
ANY	Compares a value to any value which meets the given condition
AND	Facilitates multiple conditions in the WHERE clause of an SQL statement
LIKE	Uses wildcard operators to compare similar values
BETWE EN	Searches for value(s) within the minimum and maximum values specified
EXISTS	Searches for a table row which meets a given condition
OR	Facilitates multiple conditions in the WHERE clause of SQL statements

IS NULL	Compares one value to a NULL value
UNIQUE	Searches all table rows for uniqueness
IN	Compares a value to a specified range/list of literal values
NOT	Used to reverse the meaning of the specified logical operator

The examples in this section will use the SALES_REP table with the following data:

```
+------+---------------+----------+-------------+
| ID   | EMP_NAME      | SALES    | BRANCH      |
+------+---------------+----------+-------------+
| 1001 | ALAN MARSCH   |  3000.00 | NEW YORK    |
| 1098 | NEIL BANKS    |  5400.00 | LOS ANGELES |
| 2005 | RAIN ALONZO   |  4000.00 | NEW YORK    |
| 3008 | MARK FIELDING |  3555.00 | CHICAGO     |
| 4356 | JENNER BANKS  | 14600.00 | NEW YORK    |
| 4810 | MAINE ROD     |  7000.00 | NEW YORK    |
| 5783 | JACK RINGER   |  6000.00 | CHICAGO     |
| 6431 | MARK TWAIN    | 10000.00 | LOS ANGELES |
| 7543 | JACKIE FELTS  |  3500.00 | CHICAGO     |
| 8934 | MARK GOTH     |  5400.00 | AUSTIN      |
+------+---------------+----------+-------------+
10 rows in set (0.00 sec)
```

Here are some statements that you may use to extract data from the SALES_REP table using logical operators:

```
SELECT * FROM SALES_REP WHERE SALES >= 4000.00 AND BRANCH = 'Chicago';
```

Output:

```
+------+-------------+---------+---------+
| ID   | EMP_NAME    | SALES   | BRANCH  |
+------+-------------+---------+---------+
| 5783 | JACK RINGER | 6000.00 | CHICAGO |
+------+-------------+---------+---------+
1 row in set (0.00 sec)
```

```
SELECT EMP_NAME FROM SALES_REP WHERE SALES
BETWEEN 5000.00 and 8000.00;
```

Output:

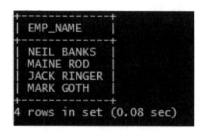

Chapter 9: SQL Functions

SQL count function

The COUNT() function is used to return the number of rows that meets the given condition.

Here's the syntax:

```
SELECT COUNT (<expression>)
FROM table_name;
```

In this statement, the expression can refer to an arithmetic operation or column name. You can also specify (*) if you want to calculate the total records stored in the table.

The examples in this section will use the data in SALES_REP table:

```
+-------+----------------+-----------+-------------+
| ID    | EMP_NAME       | SALES     | BRANCH      |
+-------+----------------+-----------+-------------+
| 1001  | ALAN MARSCH    | 3000.00   | NEW YORK    |
| 1098  | NEIL BANKS     | 5400.00   | LOS ANGELES |
| 2005  | RAIN ALONZO    | 4000.00   | NEW YORK    |
| 3008  | MARK FIELDING  | 3555.00   | CHICAGO     |
| 4356  | JENNER BANKS   | 14600.00  | NEW YORK    |
| 4810  | MAINE ROD      | 7000.00   | NEW YORK    |
| 5783  | JACK RINGER    | 6000.00   | CHICAGO     |
| 6431  | MARK TWAIN     | 10000.00  | LOS ANGELES |
| 7543  | JACKIE FELTS   | 3500.00   | CHICAGO     |
| 8934  | MARK GOTH      | 5400.00   | AUSTIN      |
+-------+----------------+-----------+-------------+
10 rows in set (0.00 sec)
```

To perform a simple count operation like calculating how many rows are in the SALES_REP table, you will enter:

```
SELECT COUNT(EMP_NAME)
FROM SALES_REP;
```

Here's the result:

You can also use (*) instead of specifying a column name:

```
SELECT COUNT(EMP_NAME)
FROM SALES_REP;
```

This statement will produce the same result because the EMP_NAME field has no NULL value. Assuming, however, that one of the fields in the EMP_NAME contains a NULL value, this would not be included in the statement that specifies EMP_NAME but will be included in the COUNT() result if you use the * symbol as parameter.

You can also use the COUNT function with the GROUP by clause. For example, if you want to calculate the number of records for every branch, you can enter this statement:

```
SELECT BRANCH, COUNT(*) FROM SALES_REP
GROUP BY BRANCH;
```

This would be the output:

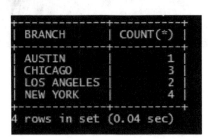

The COUNT() function can be used with DISTINCT to find the number of distinct entries. For instance, if you want to know how many distinct branches are saved in the SALES_REP table, you will enter this statement:

```
SELECT COUNT (DISTINCT BRANCH)
FROM SALES_REP;
```

It will produce this result:

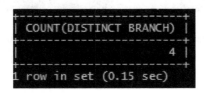

SQL AVG Function

The AVG() function calculates the average value of columns with numeric data type.

Here is the syntax:

```
SELECT AVG (<expression>)
FROM "table_name";
```

In the above statement, the expression can refer to an arithmetic operation or to a column name. Arithmetic operations can take single or multiple columns.

The examples in this section will use the SALES_REP table with this data:

```
+-------+-------------------+-------------+------------------+
| ID    | EMP_NAME          | SALES       | BRANCH           |
+-------+-------------------+-------------+------------------+
| 1001  | ALAN MARSCH       |  3000.00    | NEW YORK         |
| 1098  | NEIL BANKS        |  5400.00    | LOS ANGELES      |
| 2005  | RAIN ALONZO       |  4000.00    | NEW YORK         |
| 3008  | MARK FIELDING     |  3555.00    | CHICAGO          |
| 4356  | JENNER BANKS      | 14600.00    | NEW YORK         |
| 4810  | MAINE ROD         |  7000.00    | NEW YORK         |
| 5783  | JACK RINGER       |  6000.00    | CHICAGO          |
| 6431  | MARK TWAIN        | 10000.00    | LOS ANGELES      |
| 7543  | JACKIE FELTS      |  3500.00    | CHICAGO          |
| 8934  | MARK GOTH         |  5400.00    | AUSTIN           |
+-------+-------------------+-------------+------------------+
10 rows in set (0.00 sec)
```

In the first example, you will use the AVG() function to calculate the average sales amount. You can enter this statement:

```
SELECT AVG(Sales) FROM Sales_Rep;
```

Here's the result:

```
+-------------+
| AVG(SALES)  |
+-------------+
| 6245.500000 |
+-------------+
1 row in set (0.00 sec)
```

The figure 6245.500000 is the average of all sales data in the Sales_Rep table and it is computed by adding the Sales field and dividing the result by the number of records which, in this example, is 10 rows.

The AVG() function can be used in arithmetic operations. For example, assuming that sales tax is 6.6% of sales, you can use this statement to calculate the average sales tax figure:

```
SELECT AVG(Sales*.066) FROM Sales_Rep;
```

Here's the result:

To obtain the result, SQL had to calculate the result of the arithmetic operation 'Sales *.066' before applying the AVG function.

You can combine the AVG() function with the GROUP BY clause to get the average figure for a specified grouping. For example, assume that you want to calculate the average sales for each branch, you can enter this statement:

```
SELECT Branch, AVG(Sales) FROM Sales_Rep
GROUP BY Branch;
```

Here's the result:

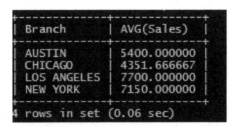

SQL ROUND Function

The ROUND() function is used to round a number to a given number of decimals or precision.

This is the syntax for SQL ROUND() function:

```
ROUND (expression, [decimal place])
```

In the above statement, the decimal place specifies the number of decimal points that will be returned. If you specify a negative number, it will round off the digit on the left of the decimal point. For instance, specifying -1 will round off the number to the nearest tens.

The examples on this section will use the Student_Grade table with the following data:

ID	Name	Grade
1	Jack Knight	87.6498
2	Daisy Poult	98.4359
3	James McDuff	97.7853
4	Alicia Stone	89.9753

Assuming that you want to round off the grades to the nearest tenths, you can enter this statement:

```
SELECT Name, ROUND (Grade, 1) Rounded_Grade
FROM Student_Grade;
```

This would be the result:

```
+----------------+---------------+
| Name           | Rounded_Grade |
+----------------+---------------+
| Jack Knight    |          87.6 |
| Daisy Poult    |          98.4 |
| James McDuff   |          97.8 |
| Alicia Stone   |          90.0 |
+----------------+---------------+
4 rows in set (0.46 sec)
```

Assuming that you want to round the grades to the nearest tens, you will use a negative parameter for the ROUND() function:

```
SELECT Name, ROUND (Grade, -1) Rounded_Grade
FROM Student_Grade;
```

Here's the result:

SQL SUM Function

The SUM() function is used to return the total for an expression.

Here's the syntax for the SUM() function:

SELECT SUM(<expression>)
FROM "table_name";

The expression parameter can refer to an arithmetic operation or a column name. Arithmetic operations may include one or more columns.

Likewise, there can be more than one column in the SELECT statement in addition to the column specified in the SUM() function. These columns should also form part of the GROUP BY clause. Here's the syntax:

SELECT column1, column2, ... columnN , SUM("columnN+1")
FROM table_name;
GROUP BY column1, column2, ... column_nameN;

For the examples in this section, you will use the SALES_REP table with the following data:

```
+------+----------------+-----------+-------------+
| ID   | EMP_NAME       | SALES     | BRANCH      |
+------+----------------+-----------+-------------+
| 1001 | ALAN MARSCH    |  3000.00  | NEW YORK    |
| 1098 | NEIL BANKS     |  5400.00  | LOS ANGELES |
| 2005 | RAIN ALONZO    |  4000.00  | NEW YORK    |
| 3008 | MARK FIELDING  |  3555.00  | CHICAGO     |
| 4356 | JENNER BANKS   | 14600.00  | NEW YORK    |
| 4810 | MAINE ROD      |  7000.00  | NEW YORK    |
| 5783 | JACK RINGER    |  6000.00  | CHICAGO     |
| 6431 | MARK TWAIN     | 10000.00  | LOS ANGELES |
| 7543 | JACKIE FELTS   |  3500.00  | CHICAGO     |
| 8934 | MARK GOTH      |  5400.00  | AUSTIN      |
+------+----------------+-----------+-------------+
10 rows in set (0.00 sec)
```

To calculate the total of all sales from the Sales_Rep, table, you will enter this statement:

```
SELECT SUM(Sales) FROM Sales_Rep;
```

This would be the result:

```
+-----------+
| SUM(Sales) |
+-----------+
|  62455.00 |
+-----------+
1 row in set (0.00 sec)
```

The figure 62455.00 represents the total of all entries in the Sales column.

To illustrate how you can use an arithmetic operation as an argument in the SUM() function, assume that you have to apply a sales tax of 6.6% on the sales figure. Here's the statement to obtain the total sales tax:

```
SELECT SUM(Sales*.066) FROM Sales_Rep;
```

You will get the following result:

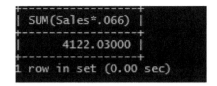

In this example, you will combine the SUM() function and the GROUP BY clause to calculate the total sales for each branch. You can use this statement:

```
SELECT Branch, SUM(Sales) FROM Sales_Rep
GROUP BY Branch;
```

Here's the result:

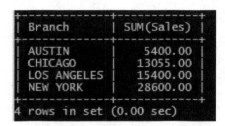

SQL MAX() Function

The MAX() function is used to obtain the largest value in a given expression.

Here's the syntax:

```
SELECT MAX (<expression>)
FROM table_name;
```

The expression parameter can be an arithmetic operation or a column name. Arithmetic operations can have multiple columns.

The SELECT statement can have one or more columns besides the column specified in the MAX() function. If this is the case, these columns will have to form part of the GROUP BY clause.

The syntax would be:

```
SELECT column1, column2, ... "columnN", MAX
(<expression>)
FROM table_name;
GROUP BY column1, column2, ... "columnN";
```

To demonstrate, you will use the table Sales_Rep with this data:

```
+------+---------------+----------+-------------+
| ID   | EMP_NAME      | SALES    | BRANCH      |
+------+---------------+----------+-------------+
| 1001 | ALAN MARSCH   |  3000.00 | NEW YORK    |
| 1098 | NEIL BANKS    |  5400.00 | LOS ANGELES |
| 2005 | RAIN ALONZO   |  4000.00 | NEW YORK    |
| 3008 | MARK FIELDING |  3555.00 | CHICAGO     |
| 4356 | JENNER BANKS  | 14600.00 | NEW YORK    |
| 4810 | MAINE ROD     |  7000.00 | NEW YORK    |
| 5783 | JACK RINGER   |  6000.00 | CHICAGO     |
| 6431 | MARK TWAIN    | 10000.00 | LOS ANGELES |
| 7543 | JACKIE FELTS  |  3500.00 | CHICAGO     |
| 8934 | MARK GOTH     |  5400.00 | AUSTIN      |
+------+---------------+----------+-------------+
10 rows in set (0.00 sec)
```

To get the highest sales amount, you will enter this statement:

```
SELECT MAX(Sales) FROM Sales_Rep;
```

Here's the result:

```
+------------+
| MAX(Sales) |
+------------+
|   14600.00 |
+------------+
1 row in set (0.08 sec)
```

To illustrate how the MAX() function is applied to an arithmetic operation, assume that you have to compute a sales tax of 6.6% on the sales figure. To get the highest sales tax figure, you will use this statement;

```
SELECT MAX(Sales*0.066) FROM Sales_Rep;
```

Here's the output:

You can combine the MAX() function with the GROUP BY clause to obtain the maximum sales value per branch. You will have to enter this statement:

```
SELECT Branch, MAX(Sales) FROM Sales_Rep
GROUP BY Branch;
```

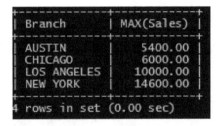

SQL MIN() Function

The MIN() function is used to obtain the lowest value in a given expression.

Here's the syntax:

```
SELECT MIN(<expression>)
FROM table_name;
```

The expression parameter can be an arithmetic operation or a column name. Arithmetic operations can also have several columns.

The SELECT statement can have one or several columns besides the column specified in the MIN() function. If this is the case, these columns will have to form part of the GROUP BY clause.

The syntax would be:

```
SELECT column1, column2, ... "columnN", MIN
(<expression>)
FROM table_name;
GROUP BY column1, column2, ... "columnN";
```

To demonstrate how the MIN() function is used in SQL, you will use the Sales_Rep table with the following data:

```
+------+---------------+----------+-------------+
| ID   | EMP_NAME      | SALES    | BRANCH      |
+------+---------------+----------+-------------+
| 1001 | ALAN MARSCH   |  3000.00 | NEW YORK    |
| 1098 | NEIL BANKS    |  5400.00 | LOS ANGELES |
| 2005 | RAIN ALONZO   |  4000.00 | NEW YORK    |
| 3008 | MARK FIELDING |  3555.00 | CHICAGO     |
| 4356 | JENNER BANKS  | 14600.00 | NEW YORK    |
| 4810 | MAINE ROD     |  7000.00 | NEW YORK    |
| 5783 | JACK RINGER   |  6000.00 | CHICAGO     |
| 6431 | MARK TWAIN    | 10000.00 | LOS ANGELES |
| 7543 | JACKIE FELTS  |  3500.00 | CHICAGO     |
| 8934 | MARK GOTH     |  5400.00 | AUSTIN      |
+------+---------------+----------+-------------+
10 rows in set (0.00 sec)
```

To get the lowest sales amount, you can use this statement:

```
SELECT MIN(Sales) FROM Sales_Rep;
```

The output would be:

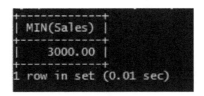

To demonstrate how the `MIN()` function is used on arithmetic operations, assume that you have to compute a sales tax of 6.6% on the sales figure. To get the lowest sales tax figure, you will use this statement;

```
SELECT MIN(Sales*0.066) FROM Sales_Rep;
```

Here's the output:

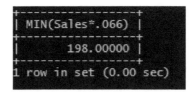

You can also use the `MIN()` function with the GROUP BY clause to calculate the minimum sales value per branch. You will have to enter this statement:

```
SELECT Branch, MIN(Sales) FROM Sales_Rep
GROUP BY Branch;
```

Here's the result:

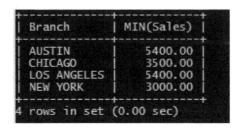

Chapter 10: Tables Modifying And Controlling

Altering table

The `ALTER TABLE` command is used to modify existing database tables. This is a powerful command that will let you change a table's name, add new fields, remove columns, edit field definitions, modify the table's storage values, and include or exclude constraints.

Here's the basic syntax for altering a table:

```
ALTER TABLE TABLE_NAME [MODIFY] [COLUMN COLUMN_NAME][DATATYPE|NULL NOT NULL]
[RESTRICT|CASCADE]
                [DROP]    [CONSTRAINT CONSTRAINT_NAME]
                [ADD]     [COLUMN] COLUMN DEFINITION
```

Changing a Table's Name

The `ALTER TABLE` command can be used with the `RENAME` function to change a table's name.

To demonstrate the use of this statement, you will use the EMPLOYEES table with the following records:

```
+----+------------+-----------+------------+----------+---------------------+
| ID | FIRST_NAME | LAST_NAME | POSITION   | SALARY   | ADDRESS             |
+----+------------+-----------+------------+----------+---------------------+
|  1 | Robert     | Page      | Clerk      | 5000.00  | 282 Patterson Avenue, Ill
inois |
|  2 | John       | Malley    | Supervisor | 7000.00  | 5 Lake View New York
|  3 | Kristen    | Johnston  | Clerk      | 4000.00  | 25 Jump Road Florida
|  4 | Jack       | Burns     | Agent      | 5000.00  | 5 Green Meadows Californi
a
|  5 | James      | Hunt      | NULL       | 7500.00  | NULL
+----+------------+-----------+------------+----------+---------------------+
```

Assuming that you want to change the EMPLOYEES table name to INVESTORS, you can easily do so with this statement:

ALTER TABLE EMPLOYEES RENAME INVESTORS;

Your table is now named INVESTORS.

Modifying Column Attributes

A column's attributes refer to the properties and behaviors of data entered in a column. You will normally set the column attributes at the time you create the table. However, you may still change one or more attributes using the ALTER TABLE command.

You may modify the following:

- Column name
- Column Data type assigned to a column
- The scale, length, or precision of a column
- Use or non-use of NULL values in a column

Renaming Columns

You may want to modify a column's name to reflect the data that they contain. For instance, since you renamed the EMPLOYEES database to INVESTORS, the column name SALARY will no longer be appropriate. You can change the column name to something like CAPITAL. Likewise, you may want to change its data type from DECIMAL to an INTEGER TYPE with a maximum of ten digits.

You can enter this statement:

```
ALTER TABLE INVESTORS CHANGE SALARY CAPITAL INT(10);
```

Here's the result:

```
+----+------------+-----------+------------+---------+----------------------------+
| ID | FIRST_NAME | LAST_NAME | POSITION   | CAPITAL | ADDRESS                    |
+----+------------+-----------+------------+---------+----------------------------+
|  1 | Robert     | Page      | Clerk      |    5000 | 282 Patterson Avenue, Illinois |
|  2 | John       | Malley    | Supervisor |    7000 | 5 Lake View New York       |
|  3 | Kristen    | Johnston  | Clerk      |    4000 | 25 Jump Road Florida       |
|  4 | Jack       | Burns     | Agent      |    5000 | 5 Green Meadows California  |
|  5 | James      | Hunt      | NULL       |    7500 | NULL                       |
+----+------------+-----------+------------+---------+----------------------------+
5 rows in set (0.01 sec)
```

Deleting a Column

The column Position is no longer applicable at this point. You can drop the column using this statement:

```
ALTER TABLE INVESTORS
DROP COLUMN Position;
```

Here's the updated INVESTORS table:

```
+----+------------+-----------+---------+-----------------------------+
| ID | FIRST_NAME | LAST_NAME | CAPITAL | ADDRESS                     |
+----+------------+-----------+---------+-----------------------------+
|  1 | Robert     | Page      |    5000 | 282 Patterson Avenue, Illinois |
|  2 | John       | Malley    |    7000 | 5 Lake View New York        |
|  3 | Kristen    | Johnston  |    4000 | 25 Jump Road Florida        |
|  4 | Jack       | Burns     |    5000 | 5 Green Meadows California   |
|  5 | James      | Hunt      |    7500 | NULL                        |
+----+------------+-----------+---------+-----------------------------+
5 rows in set (0.00 sec)
```

Adding a New Column

Since you're now working on a different set of data, you may decide to add another column to make the data on the INVESTORS table more relevant. You can add a column that will store the number of stocks owned by each investor. You may name the new column as STOCKS. This column will accept integers up to 9 digits.

You can use this statement to add the STOCKS column:

```
ALTER TABLE INVESTORS ADD STOCKS INT(9);
```

Here's the updated INVESTOR'S table:

```
+----+------------+-----------+---------+-----------------------------+--------+
| ID | FIRST_NAME | LAST_NAME | CAPITAL | ADDRESS                     | STOCKS |
+----+------------+-----------+---------+-----------------------------+--------+
|  1 | Robert     | Page      | 5000.00 | 282 Patterson Avenue, Illinois | NULL |
|  2 | John       | Malley    | 7000.00 | 5 Lake View New York        | NULL   |
|  3 | Kristen    | Johnston  | 4000.00 | 25 Jump Road Florida        | NULL   |
|  4 | Jack       | Burns     | 5000.00 | 5 Green Meadows California   | NULL   |
|  5 | James      | Hunt      | 7500.00 | NULL                        | NULL   |
+----+------------+-----------+---------+-----------------------------+--------+
```

Modifying an Existing Column without Changing its Name

You may also combine the ALTER TABLE command with the MODIFY keyword to change the data type and specifications of a table. To demonstrate, you can use the following statement to modify the data type of the column CAPITAL from an INT type to a DECIMAL type with up to 9 digits and two decimal numbers.

ALTER TABLE INVESTORS MODIFY CAPITAL DECIMAL(9,2) NOT NULL;

By this time, you may be curious to see the column names and attributes of the INVESTORS table. You can use the 'SHOW COLUMNS' statement to display the table's structure. Enter the following statement:

SHOW COLUMNS FROM INVESTORS;

Here's a screenshot of the result:

```
+-------------+-------------+------+-----+---------+-------+
| Field       | Type        | Null | Key | Default | Extra |
+-------------+-------------+------+-----+---------+-------+
| ID          | int(6)      | NO   |     | 0       |       |
| FIRST_NAME  | varchar(35) | NO   |     | NULL    |       |
| LAST_NAME   | varchar(35) | NO   |     | NULL    |       |
| CAPITAL     | decimal(9,2)| NO   |     | NULL    |       |
| ADDRESS     | varchar(50) | YES  |     | NULL    |       |
| STOCKS      | int(9)      | YES  |     | NULL    |       |
+-------------+-------------+------+-----+---------+-------+
6 rows in set (0.00 sec)
```

You will also get the same results with this statement:

DESC INVESTORS;

Rules to Remember when Using ALTER TABLE

• Adding Columns to a Database Table

When adding a new column, bear in mind that you can't add a column with a NOT NULL attribute to a table with existing data. You will generally specify a column to be NOT NULL to indicate that it will hold a value. Adding a NOT NULL column with contradict the constraint if the existing data don't have values for a new column.

• Modifying Fields/Columns

You should pay close attention to the following rules when modifying current database column:

1. You can easily modify the data type of a column.
2. You can always increase the length of a column but you may only decrease the length of a column if it is equal to or shorter than the desired column length.
3. You can increase the number of digits that numeric data types will hold but you will only be able to decrease it if the largest number of digits stored by a table is equal to or lower than the desired number of digits.
4. You can increase or decrease the decimal places of numeric data types as long as they don't exceed the maximum allowable decimal places.

Deleting and modifying tables can result to loss of valuable information if not handled properly. Hence, be extremely careful when you're executing the ALTER TABLE and DROP TABLE statements.

Deleting Tables

The DROP TABLE command is used to remove a table and its definitions from a database. Dropping a table will also remove its data, associated index, triggers, constraints, and permission data. You should be careful when using this statement.

Here's the syntax::

 DROP TABLE table_name;

For example, if you want to delete the INVESTORS TABLE from the xyzcompany database, you may use this statement:

```
DROP TABLE INVESTORS;
```

The DROP TABLE command effectively removed the INVESTORS table from the current database.

If you try to access the INVESTORS table with this command:

```
SELECT* FROM INVESTORS;
```

SQL will return an error like this;

```
ERROR 1146 (42S02): Table 'xyzcompany.investors' doesn't exist
```

Combining and joining tables

You can combine data from several tables if a common field exists between them. The JOIN statement is used to perform this action.

SQL supports several types of JOIN operations:

INNER JOIN

The INNER JOIN, or simply JOIN, is the most commonly used type of JOIN. It displays the rows when the tables to be joined have a matching field.

Here's the syntax:

```
SELECT column_name(s)
FROM table1
INNER JOIN table2
ON table1.column_name=table2.column_name;
```

In this variation, the JOIN clause is used instead of INNER JOIN.

```
SELECT column_name(s)
FROM table1
JOIN table2
ON table1.column_name=table2.column_name;
```

LEFT JOIN

The LEFT JOIN operation returns all left table rows with the matching right table rows. If no match is found, the right side returns NULL.

Here's the syntax for LEFT JOIN:

```
SELECT column_name(s)
FROM table1
LEFT JOIN table2
ON table1.column_name=table2.column_name;
```

In some database systems, the keyword LEFT OUTER JOIN is used instead of LEFT JOIN. Here's the syntax for this variation:

SELECT column_name(s)
FROM table1
LEFT OUTER JOIN table2
ON table1.column_name=table2.column_name;

RIGHT JOIN

This JOIN operation returns all right table rows with the matching left table rows. If no match is found, the left side returns NULL.

Here's the syntax for this operation:

SELECT column_name(s)
FROM table1
RIGHT JOIN table2
ON table1.column_name=table2.column_name;

In some database systems, the RIGHT OUTER JOIN is used instead of LEFT JOIN. Here's the syntax for this variation:

SELECT column_name(s)
FROM table1
RIGHT OUTER JOIN table2
ON table1.column_name=table2.column_name;

FULL OUTER JOIN

This JOIN operation will display all rows when at least one table meets the condition. It combines the results from both RIGHT and LEFT join operations.

Here's the syntax:

```
SELECT column_name(s)
FROM table1
FULL OUTER JOIN table2
ON table1.column_name=table2.column_name;
```

To demonstrate the JOIN operation in SQL, you will use the tables Branch_Sales and Branch_Location:

Branch_Sales Table

Branch	Product_ID	Sales
New York	101	7500.00
Los Angeles	102	6450.00
Chicago	101	1560.00
Philadelphia	101	1980.00
Denver	102	3500.00
Seattle	101	2500.00
Detroit	102	1450.00

Location Table

Region	Branch
East	New York City
East	Chicago
East	Philadelphia
East	Detroit
West	Los Angeles
West	Denver
West	Seattle

The objective is to fetch the sales by region. The Location table contains the data on regions and branches while the Branch_Sales table holds the sales data for each branch. To find the sales per region, you will need to combine the data from the Location and Branch_Sales tables. Notice that these tables have a common field, the Branch. This field links the two tables.

The following statement will demonstrate how you can link these two tables by using table aliases:

```
SELECT A1.Region Region, SUM(A2.Sales) Sales
FROM Location A1, Branch_Sales A2
WHERE A1.Branch = A2.Branch
GROUP BY A1.Region;
```

This would be the result:

```
+---------+-----------+
| Region  | Sales     |
+---------+-----------+
| East    |  4990.00  |
| West    | 12450.00  |
+---------+-----------+
2 rows in set (0.12 sec)
```

In the first two lines, the statement tells SQL to select the fields 'Region' from the Location table and the total of the 'Sales' field from the Branch_Sales table. The statement uses table aliases. The 'Region' field was aliased as Region while the sum of the SALES field was aliased as SALES.

Table aliasing is the practice of using a temporary name for a table or a table column. Using aliases helps make statements more readable and concise. For example, if you opt not to use a table alias for the first line, you would have used the following statement to achieve the same result:

```
SELECT Location.Region Region,
SUM(Branch_Sales.Sales) SALES
```

Alternatively, you can specify a join between two tables by using the JOIN and ON keywords. For instance, using these keywords, the query would be:

```
SELECT A1.Region REGION, SUM(A2.Sales) SALES
FROM Location A1
JOIN Branch_Sales A2
ON A1.Branch = A2.Branch
GROUP BY A1.Region;
```

The query would produce an identical result:

Using Inner Join

An inner join displays rows when there is one or more matches on two tables. To demonstrate, you will use the following tables:

Branch_Sales table

Branch	Product_ID	Sales
New York	101	7500.00
Philadelphia	101	1980.00
Denver	102	3500.00
Seattle	101	2500.00
Detroit	102	1450.00

Location_table

Region	Branch
East	New York
East	Chicago
East	Philadelphia

East	Detroit
West	Los Angeles
West	Denver
West	Seattle

The objective of the query is to fetch the sales data per branch and only for branches that are listed in the Branch_Sales table. You can achieve this by using the INNER JOIN statement.

You can enter the following:

```
SELECT A1.Branch BRANCH, SUM(A2.Sales) SALES
FROM Location A1
INNER JOIN Branch_Sales A2
ON A1.Branch = A2.Branch
GROUP BY A1.Branch;
```

This would be the result:

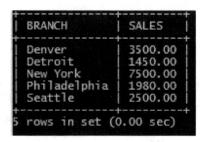

Take note that by using the INNER JOIN, only the branches with records in the Branch_Sales report were included in the results even though you are actually applying the SELECT statement on the Location table. The 'Chicago' and 'Los Angeles' branches were excluded because there are no records for these branches in the Branch_Sales table.

Using Outer Join

In the previous example, you have used the Inner Join to combine tables with common rows. In some cases, you may need to select all elements of a table whether or not they have a matching record in the second table. The OUTER JOIN command is used for this purpose.

The example for the OUTER JOIN will use the same tables used for INNER JOIN: the Branch_Sales table and Location_table.

This time, you want a list of sales figures for all stores. A regular join would have excluded Chicago and Los Angeles because these branches were not part of the Branch_Sales table. You will want, therefore, to do an OUTER JOIN.

Here's the statement:

```
SELECT A1.Branch, SUM(A2.Sales) SALES
FROM Location A1, Branch_Sales A2
WHERE A1.Branch = A2.Branch (+)
GROUP BY A1.Branch;
```

Take note that the Outer Join syntax is database-dependent. The above statement uses the Oracle syntax.

Here's the result:

Branch	Sales
Chicago	NULL
Denver	3500.00
Detroit	1450.00
Los Angeles	NULL
New York	7500.00
Philadelphia	1980.00
Seattle	2500.00

When combining tables, be aware that some JOIN syntax will have different results across database systems. To maximize this powerful database feature, it is imporant to read the RDBMS documentation.

Conclusion

Thank you again for purchasing this book, I hope you enjoyed reading it as much as I enjoyed writing it for you!

Finally, if you enjoyed this book I'd like to ask you to leave a review for my book on Amazon, it would be greatly appreciated!

All the best and good luck,